PRACTICAL
PERFECTION

Smart strategies for an excellent life

KELLY EXETER

Published in Australia by Swish Publishing,
Perth, Western Australia.

www.swishpublishing.com.au

National Library of Australia
Cataloguing-in-Publication entry

Author: Exeter, Kelly M., 1977- author.

Title: Practical Perfection: smart strategies for an
excellent life / Kelly Exeter.

ISBN: 978-0-9924416-3-0 (paperback)

Notes: Includes bibliographical references.

Subjects: Self-consciousness (Awareness). Self-acceptance.
Self-Actualization (Psychology). Life Skills.

Dewey Number: 158.1

Printed in the United States of America
First Edition

Cover Design, Book Design & Layout: Swish Design
Author photo: Robyn Petta

For Bernadette—
who is never afraid to ask me hard questions and
point out when I'm missing the obvious.

CONTENTS

PRACTICAL PERFECTION

Smart strategies for an excellent life

KELLY EXETER

INTRODUCTION

"I think you're being too hard on yourself."

Ever heard those words? I certainly have. Anyone who has high expectations of themselves has.

Always well-meaning. Often true. Seldom helpful at the time.

Because *of course* we're hard on ourselves! How does one achieve anything in life without setting high standards and then working our butts off to meet them?

Striving to meet these standards does tend to come with some pitfalls however. For a very long time, these three things were the story of my life:

- Burnout
- Overwhelm
- That feeling of being a hamster on a wheel.

So while I got to tick lots of boxes and strike lots of things off lists, all of the above meant I wasn't being the person I wanted to be.

Constantly tired and irritable? Tick.

Always vague and distracted? Tick.

Completely unable to sit still and just relax? Tick.

And that was *before* I had kids.

Some people say having kids killed their ambition. Not me. Having kids *added* to them. Now, as well as wanting to hit all my personal goals *and* be an amazing wife/daughter/sister/boss/friend, I also wanted to be a kick arse mother.

Except I suddenly had a lot less time to achieve it all.

So it will come as no surprise to hear that 18 months after my first child was born I had a complete breakdown. All that striving and holding myself to unrealistic standards didn't so much tip me over the edge as hurl me into a deep, dark hole of stress, anxiety and depression.

I tried every strategy and tactic I knew to claw my way out of that hole. But in the end I succumbed, completely losing myself, my confidence, and any sense of who I was.

So what got me out of the hole? Well, I became *very* self-aware (therapy will do that for you), and this allowed me to notice how I kept repeating certain patterns of behaviour. Once I started seeing these patterns in myself, I also began seeing them in the highly-driven people I tended to surround myself with.

We were all constantly flirting with overwhelm and burnout. We seemed to think if we weren't right on the edge, then we weren't pushing hard enough. Whenever a tiny bit of space opened up in our lives, we had to fill that space immediately. And yet we would complain how we always felt like hamsters on a wheel—running our little butts off but getting nowhere.

What was driving this behaviour? More often than not it was our pursuit of perfection.

WHAT DOES PERFECTIONISM LOOK LIKE?

When we think of perfectionism, we tend to think of people who need to be perfect at *everything* they do. (That's why I've never thought of myself as a perfectionist—there's plenty of stuff I can be half-arsed about!)

But in reality, perfectionism can present itself in a number of different ways. Researchers Paul Hewitt and Gordon Flett offer three sub-scales of perfectionism[1]:

- **Self-oriented perfectionists** adhere to strict standards while maintaining strong motivation to attain perfection and avoid failure. They also engage in stringent self-evaluation.

- **Other-oriented perfectionists** set unrealistic standards for significant others (e.g. partners, children, co-workers), coupled with a stringent evaluation of others' performances.

- **Socially-prescribed perfectionists** believe others hold unrealistic expectations for their behaviour (which they feel they can't live up to). And they experience external pressure to be perfect, believing that others evaluate them critically.

So it appears I'm a self-oriented perfectionist. (And the fact you're reading this book means you're probably one too.)

But it's not all bad news. A 2005 study by Jeffrey Kilbert, Jennifer Langhinrichsen-Rohling and Motoko Saito found that:

> ". . . self-oriented perfectionists are those who derive a sense of pleasure from their labours and efforts, which in turn enhances their self-esteem and motivation to succeed and eventually helps them to develop a sense of control over their environment."[2]

This finding is important in the context of this book. Why? Because it reflects where I have gotten to with my own brand of self-oriented perfectionism: a place where I feel like I'm in control of my life (as much as anyone can be) and thriving as a person instead of constantly teetering on the edge of overwhelm and burnout.

How did I get here? Well, I developed a framework for myself.

THE PRACTICAL PERFECTION FRAMEWORK

The first thing I need to do here is define the word 'striver' because I'm going to be using it a lot in this book. In my experience there are two types:

1. Your typically Type A, highly-driven, achievement-junkie.

2. People who don't feel they fit into the category above, yet expect a lot of themselves and are constantly endeavouring to meet those expectations.

When I use the word 'striver' in this book, I am referring to both.

Now that I've got that clear, let me share with you one big thing I learned in therapy: we can't really change the aspects of our personality that are hardwired into us. Once a striver, always a striver.

But we *can* become more self-aware. We can learn what things are stopping us from living our best life, and develop strategies to manage those things.

When I started paying attention to what was going on in my life, I found that to feel happy, content and fulfilled, I needed three things to be present:

- **Passions:** things that got me out of bed in the morning with a smile on my face.

- **Priorities:** knowing what actually mattered most to me, and then making the conscious decision to focus hard on those and let go of the rest.

- **Productivity:** the ability to get things started *and* finished.

Looking back, I can see that whenever one of those three key things was lacking in my life, problems arose.

For example:

Productivity + Priorities = Yes, I got a lot of stuff done. But without any of my Passions, I **burnt out** because there was nothing to buffer the stress and anxiety that tends to go with the striver life.

Passions + Productivity = I was doing a lot of things I loved and getting a lot done. But without Prioritisation life felt out of control and I was in a permanent state of **overwhelm** because every opportunity or request seemed like a good idea.

Priorities + Passions = I had lots of ideas, and enough time and drive to chase after every one of them. But I never seemed to finish anything before moving on to the next. In the absence of Productivity I was extremely busy, but not actually achieving anything– the proverbial **hamster on a wheel**.

But when all three were present I entered a **zone** of what I call **Practical Perfection**–a place where I felt content, fulfilled, and able to deal with life's (inevitable) challenges as they arose.

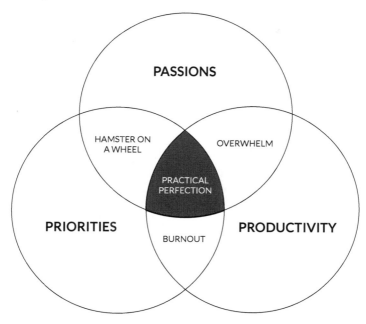

And that whole 'zone' thing is one of my favourite aspects of the Practical Perfection Framework. Those of us with perfectionist tendencies usually strive for a **'sweet spot'** in life–a place where all the planets align and we feel like we're 'there'. Unfortunately, that state of perfect balance only lasts for a moment before things inevitably shift and the moment is gone. How utterly depressing and de-motivating!

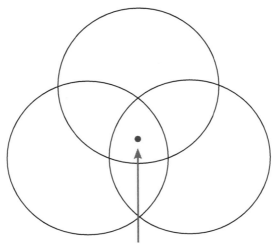

What we tend to aim for: a sweet spot

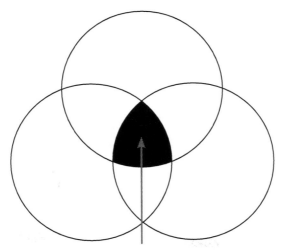

What we should aim for: to get 'centred' and
operate within the optimal 'zone'

Entering a '**zone**', however, is much more achievable. And whenever you slip out of the middle zone of Practical Perfection into one of the other areas (which will happen, because–life!), the framework tells you what you need to get centred again.

- **On the brink of burnout?** Time to inject some more **Passions** back into your life.

- **Overwhelmed?** Time to get on top of your **Priorities**.

- **Feeling like a hamster on a wheel?** Time to put your head down and get **Productive**.

If you're a self-oriented perfectionist like me, then you probably like to feel in control of your life (as much as that's possible). The Practical Perfection Framework gives you both the feeling of control you crave *and* a strong foundation for building an excellent life.

WHAT DOES AN EXCELLENT LIFE LOOK LIKE?

Well, one thing's for sure, it's not the 'perfect' life because there's no such thing. And chances are everyone's 'excellent' life is slightly different. But for me (and hopefully for you), an excellent life is one where:

- You get to achieve what you want *without* the constant stress and overwhelm people who set high standards for themselves tend to experience.

- You have time and space to be good to those closest to you.

- You have time and space to be good to the world.

- You have time and space to be good to *yourself.*

In the past, whenever the pressure was on I'd fall back into the same old behavioural patterns. And those patterns always led me down the paths of overwhelm, burnout and feeling like a hamster on a wheel.

These days, the Practical Perfection Framework warns me when my feet are heading down any of those paths much earlier, and tells me what I need to do to 'return to centre'.

HOW THIS BOOK WILL WORK

This book has three main sections: **Burnout**, **Overwhelm** and **Hamster on a Wheel**. Each section talks about how we end up feeling that particular way, and how we can use Passions, Priorities and Productivity respectively as antidotes.

The final section of the book will demonstrate how tying all of the above together with one vital, common thread will help you achieve an excellent life.

If you've just picked up this book I recommend reading it from cover to cover, as each section builds on the one before. But once you've finished it you can open the appropriate section whenever you need practical tips to deal with a specific 'thing'.

Speaking of practical ...

Everything I talk about in this book I've tried myself. None of what I share is 'in theory'. I know these things work, and not just for me. I've shared most of these ideas on my blog, and dozens of people have said my methods also helped them achieve significant breakthroughs.

I sincerely hope some significant breakthroughs are lying in the coming pages for you too.

Let's get started.

SECTION 1: BURNOUT

> **Priorities + Productivity in the absence of Passions**
> = BURNOUT

A conversation with my husband.

"I want to sell the business. Or shut it down. I don't care which."

"What? No! It's a good business. Why?"

"I just can't do it anymore. I hate it. I haven't created a business. I've created a job for myself. And I hate my job."

"Kel, I get that. But there are things you can do–"

"I've. Tried. Every. Thing. Everything. I've lost count of how many times friends have asked, 'How are things going?' and I've said, 'Not so good, but I'm doing x or y and that's going to make things better'. But things aren't getting better. I hate my life, Ant. And I hate the person this business has turned me into."

"Okay. Well, here's a thought. Why don't you take a break from the business and let me run things?"

"What? You're a teacher! You can't run a design business! And you won't look after my clients the way I look after them."

"Kel, you're talking about either walking away from the business or shutting it down. So you're clearly a bit beyond caring about your clients. What difference does it make whether it's me 'not looking after your clients properly' or someone else?"

"..."

"Am I right?"

"Yes, okay. You're right. I just don't care anymore. If you want to run the business, go right ahead. I'm done."

What does burnout look like? The Merriam-Webster dictionary describes it as:

> "Exhaustion of physical or emotional strength or motivation usually as a result of prolonged stress."

How do you know you've reached the point of burnout? A clue lies in these five words:

> "I just don't care anymore."

When I was having that conversation with my husband I was very much the dictionary definition: stressed out of my ever-loving mind, emotionally shattered, and exhibiting a complete lack of motivation and zest for life.

How did I get to that point?

The same way most people do: slowly and insidiously.

When I flipped the calendar over to 2009 I'd been running

my own business for three years and loving it. I loved being in control of my own destiny and who I worked with, and the business was growing rapidly. I only had one small concern—I was pregnant.

Unfortunately, spending all my time running the business, managing staff and doing client work meant I hadn't set up the business to run without me. I had designers to take care of my client work, but everything else—the accounting, marketing and general shit kicking—still fell to me.

I ended up working throughout my pregnancy without taking a single day off. The day after my son was born I was sending out invoices from my hospital bed. My clients were horrified, but if I didn't send them out we wouldn't get paid. And I had three staff (including me) drawing a wage from the business.

Those early days weren't too bad. As soon as my new baby fell asleep I'd jump on my laptop and take care of business. But as the months wore on I started to wear down.

Ironically, it was my Productivity and ability to Prioritise that kept me going for as long as I did. If I was on my laptop I knew exactly what needed to be done while my son was asleep (thank God he was a reliable sleeper), and I powered through my work like nobody's business.

People constantly marvelled at what I achieved as a first-time mother. I ran our household, dealt with our builder (yes, we were also building a house at the time), ran my business, and even found time to exercise and get my pre-baby body back.

Yep, it looked like I had everything under control.

Except I didn't. That's when I had my breakdown.

As we saw in the dictionary definition of burnout, prolonged stress is generally the main driver. And certainly, that is what got me in the end. But some people seemed to be able to deal with huge amounts of stress without ever burning out. 'Why was that?', I wondered.

Here's Emma Isaacs, CEO of Business Chicks:

> "With four kids aged six and under, running a global business and a recent re-location to the US, there are some days where it can feel impossible for me to get out of bed ... I couldn't do what I do without control of my mindset, belief and commitment; knowing that what I do has the power to change the world in some way. As an entrepreneur, you build a business for that reason alone—you won't get far if you're doing it for money, ego or any other reason. At the end of the day it's about that passion."

LET'S TALK ABOUT PASSIONS

Admit it: when you saw the word 'passion' above, you rolled your eyes, didn't you? Probably because as well as being something that's seen as nice-to-have-but-not-really-essential we subconsciously link it with 'work'. I mostly blame Apple founder Steve Jobs for this. He once famously said:

> "Your work is going to fill a large part of your life, and the only way to be truly satisfied is to do what you believe is great work. And the only way to do great work is to love what you do. If you haven't found it yet, keep looking. Don't settle."

William MacAskill points out another reason for the link between passion and work in an article for 99u.com:

> "We have more freedom now to choose our careers than at any point in history. Maybe that's why talk of 'following your passion' has become so popular, allowing us to indulge in fantasies of pursuing what we currently enjoy full-time—and getting paid well for it."[3]

Cal Newport also talks about why the call to 'follow your passion' is so attractive in an interview with The Minimalists:

> "It's appealing because it's both simple and daring. It tells you that you have a calling, and if you can discover it and muster the courage to follow it, your working life will be fantastic. A big, bold move that changes everything: this is a powerful storyline."[4]

I'm sure every striver has been caught up in these storylines at some point in their life. And all in the pursuit of this:

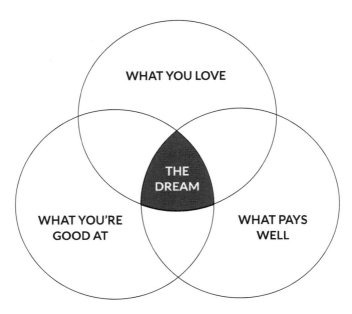

Yep, a lot of us have pursued that magical state of 'Do what you love and you'll never work another day in your life again' and come up short. No wonder people flinch whenever I mention the word 'passion'.

HOW I DEFINE 'PASSIONS'

To me, 'passion' has nothing to do with work. I believe it's something—anything—that gives you a gentle squeeze in the stomach. It's something that gets you out of bed in the morning with a smile on your face and puts a sparkle in your eye. When you talk about it to others, you feel energised and alive.

It's also important to know this when it comes to passion: we all have more than one. That's another reason the whole 'Do what you love and you'll never work another day in your life' mantra gets it wrong. It assumes there's this 'one thing' out there for all of us, and if we can just identify it we'll be happy.

But there is no 'one thing'. There are lots of things!

As an example, here's a list of my Passions:

Wellness

Fitness

Creativity

Competition

Simplicity

Effective communication

Achieving my potential

Helping others achieve their potential

Productivity

My family

Learning

Connecting people

Kindness

Achievement

Recognition

As you can see, some of these are abstract concepts. Others are obvious (who isn't passionate about their family?). And I've even been fortunate enough to make money from some of them.

It's important to note there is no 'one thing' in there. When I'm at my best as a person, I'm nurturing a combination of the above. And at different times in my life, I'll focus on some of them more than others.

That's the real beauty of our Passions—the way they can come in and out of our lives as and when we make room for them. And when we *do* make room for them we go to bed each night with satisfaction, and wake up each morning with excitement.

HOW DO PASSIONS PREVENT BURNOUT?

When we're stressed and stretched for a long time, we start feeling resentment towards other people because they all seem to be happy and we're not. Seeing them enjoying themselves and doing stuff they love makes us feel bitter about not having the same enjoyment in our own life.

This can lead to a sense of powerlessness and despondency. It feels like we can't control our lives, and are trapped in the situation we're in. And because we feel trapped it seems like we don't have choices, which further increases the feeling of resentment.

It's a horrible cycle to get into, and it's easy to see how it can quickly lead you down the path of emotional exhaustion and complete lack of motivation.

But finding the time to nurture our Passions:

- makes us happy
- removes those insidious feelings of resentment and bitterness
- lets us feel we can control something in our life.

Again you'll notice I keep saying 'Passions', and not 'passion'. Having more than one passion is important because if you spend your days pursuing a single passion like:

- The serial entrepreneur who has ten ideas every minute and never switches their brain off,
- The stay-at-home-parent who takes huge pride in running a tight ship on the home front while also being ever-available to their kids,
- The Olympic volleyball player who spends 30 hours a week training for their sport and 30 more thinking about it,

then you're just as likely to experience burnout as someone who isn't nurturing any of their Passions at all.

Nurturing multiple Passions at any one time takes the pressure off a single passion when it comes to stress relief. Here's how our potential burnout candidates from above can better mitigate against the effects of stress:

- The serial entrepreneur might also be passionate about competition and learning. Doing a weekly running event and ensuring she reads for ten minutes every night before going to sleep are both great ways to take her mind off work.

- The stay-at-home-parent? He might be passionate about body building and connecting like-minded people. So he could start a blog, and use it to share training tips and create an online community. Imagine the kick he'd get out of people in that community helping each other in the comments and making arrangements to meet up in real life.

- Meanwhile, the Olympic volleyball player could be a huge movie buff. Meeting friends at the cinema every Tuesday night to catch the latest flick, or going to someone's house to revisit an old classic would certainly be a nice break from replaying that moment where they lost the last game for their team on high repeat in their head.

Here's what was going on when I reached the point of burnout:

- I was passionate about *my family*, but I was too stressed out to be fully present around them.

- I was passionate about *good health and wellness*, but my daily exercise habit was starting to slip in favour of getting more work done. My diet was also poor, and my mental health was in tatters.

- I was passionate about *helping others*, but at the time I could barely help myself much less anyone else.

- I was a passionate *creator*, but at the time I felt I wasn't so much creating as churning out sub-standard stuff under huge time pressures.

And the worst thing about it all? I *knew* what my Passions were. I just wasn't making time for them.

But what if you're not like me? What if you genuinely have no idea what things light you up in life?

EIGHT WAYS TO IDENTIFY YOUR PASSIONS

Identify your Passions #1:
Open your eyes

I can't find anyone who explains this better than Mark Manson. So please excuse the language and listen to what he says to the hundreds of people who have asked him for help on this topic:

"You already found your passion, you're just ignoring it. Seriously, you're awake 16 hours a day, what the fuck do you do with your time? You're doing something, obviously. You're talking about something. There's some topic or activity or idea that dominates a significant amount of your free

time, your conversations, your web browsing, and it dominates them without you consciously pursuing it or looking for it.

It's right there in front of you, you're just avoiding it. For whatever reason, you're avoiding it."[5]

Identify your Passions #2: Understand yourself better

Another way to find out what your Passions might be is to try some personality typing. Some people love this stuff, and some people hate it. Personally I'm in the 'love' camp because it helped me understand and better accept certain aspects of my personality.

For years I tried to overcome my quietness, inflexibility around daily routines, and the fact that having to follow any kind of instructions makes my brain want to explode. I thought all these things made me a bad person and were flaws that needed to be overcome.

Then I did some personality typing, and discovered those traits are hardwired into me.

After that I became a lot more self-accepting, and learned to work with my strengths instead of getting angry at myself for being too 'weak' to properly address my perceived 'flaws'.

There are a lot of ways to determine your personality type. Here are four of the more popular tests, and while they can be expensive you can often find free versions on the Internet:

- StrengthsFinder 2.0
- DiSC Profile®
- Sally Hogshead's Fascination Advantage Assessment
- Myers-Briggs Type Indicator (MBTI®)

My personal favourite is the MBTI. It taught me that my particular personality type (INFJ) is full of contradictions. The Introvert (I) in me needs to be alone to recharge, but the Feeler (F) side of me loves deep and intense connections with people. And while the Intuitive (N) side of me loves taking a big picture view of things and doesn't like getting bogged down in details and processes, the Judger (J) in me needs to be highly organised. No wonder I feel at odds with myself so often!

INFJs are also hard-core idealists and have a need to help the world. Most specifically, INFJs love helping people bring order to their lives.

Finding out all this (and more) gave me an intimate understanding of what drives me and makes me happy. It also gave me huge clues as to where my Passions lay, and how I could make room for those Passions in my life without depleting my energy levels.

For example, as much as I love feeling connected to people, in-person human interaction drains me very quickly. So my capacity for helping people that way is limited. But helping people through books and blog posts, podcasting and reaching out on social media is a different story. I have almost unlimited energy for that so that's what I tend to stick to.

Want some similar insights into your personality type? In 2013 I collaborated with Carly Toomey from Type-Coach (type-coach.com) on a series of blog posts identifying what makes each personality type particularly 'buzzy', complete with case studies of each type. You can check out that series of blog posts by visiting this page on my website: *kellyexeter.com.au/personality*.

Identify your Passions #3:
Ask yourself, 'What am I willing to experience a lot of discomfort for?'

Are you prepared to stand in line for hours to get the latest Apple device before everyone else? Will you get up at 5am every day for six months to train for an Ironman triathlon? Do you think nothing of spending eight hours researching, writing and editing a single blog post before hitting 'publish'?

These are all clues. But what they suggest about you isn't always what you think. For example:

- The girl who lines up for the first crack at the latest iPhone isn't necessarily passionate about Apple products. She's probably more passionate about being an early adopter and staying 'ahead of the curve'.

- The guy training for the Ironman triathlon is probably more passionate about pushing physical boundaries than he is about triathlon itself.

- The blogger who spends eight hours on a single post could be more passionate about the *ideas* they're trying to communicate than the actual writing.

Identify your Passions #4:
Ask yourself, 'What am I curious about?'

Here's Elizabeth Gilbert (author of *Eat, Pray, Love*). In her wonderful creative manifesto, *Big Magic*, she urges us to follow our curiosity and see where it leads us. The beauty of curiosity is that it:

"... only ever asks one simple question: "Is there anything you're interested in?" Anything? Even a tiny bit? No matter how mundane or small? The answer need not set your life on fire, or make you quit your job, or force you to change your religion, or send you into a fugue state; it just has to capture your attention for a moment. But in that moment, if you can pause and identify even one tiny speck of interest in something, then curiosity will ask you to turn your head a quarter of an inch and look at the thing a wee bit closer. Do it. It's a clue. It might seem like nothing, but it's a clue. Follow that clue. Trust it. See where curiosity will lead you next. Then follow the next clue, and the next, and the next. Remember, it doesn't have to be a voice in the desert; it's just

a harmless little scavenger hunt. Following that scavenger hunt of curiosity can lead you to amazing, unexpected places."[6]

For a lot of people this focus on 'curiosity' really hits the mark as it removes the sense of desperation that tends to go with finding your Passions.

Identify your Passions #5:
Ask yourself, 'What am I good at?'

Oliver Emberton believes passion comes from success. He says:

"All of our emotions exist for good reason. We feel hunger to ensure we don't starve. We feel full to ensure we don't burst. And we feel passion to ensure we concentrate our efforts on things that reward us the most.

Imagine you start a dance class. You find it easy. You realise you're getting better than others, and fast. That rising excitement you feel is your passion, and that passion makes you come back for more, improving your skills, and compounding your strengths."[7]

We're all good at something, or know a lot about something. Unfortunately, we tend to think that because *we're* good at that thing or know about it then everyone else must be good at it or know a lot about it too. But nine times out of ten they aren't, and they don't.

A good way to identify what you're good at (stuff you might be taking for granted) is to ask your friends and family. You might also want to pay attention to the things people come to you for advice about.

They're all clues.

Identify your Passions #6:
Ask yourself, 'What's one thing that always lifts my mood when I do it?'

The next time you feel particularly 'buzzy' or 'high on life', pay attention. What are you doing? And why does it make you feel that way?

Again, the answer is usually beyond the obvious.

For example, I always feel really high after speaking or giving a presentation. Is it the act of speaking that makes me buzzy, or the opportunity to share my ideas with a large and captive audience?

When I finish a running race and I have a big, silly grin from ear to ear, is it the act of running that excites me or the thrill of competition?

By taking the time to look below the surface of your excitement you'll find there are multiple ways to get that 'passion hit'. It was exciting to find out there were other ways I could experience the thrill of competition besides running, and that public speaking was just one of many ways I could get my ideas out into the world.

Identify your Passions #7:
Ask yourself, 'What can't my friends shut me up about?'

We've all experienced that situation where we're chatting with friends and they all get a look on their face that says, "Here we go. She's on her soapbox again".

Don't let their soapbox 'comment', or the fact their eyes have started glazing over, deflate you. Own it, and then find a more receptive audience.

I have a real passion for self-improvement. But it's not something my friends or family really care about. That's why I have a blog—so I can share my ideas and passions with people who *do* care.

Identify your Passions #8: Ask yourself, 'What legacy do I want to leave this world?'

In his stunning essay *The Moral Bucket List* written for *The New York Times*, David Brooks looks at people who've achieved a real sense of inner peace and contentment and tries to divine the difference between them and him:

> "Commencement speakers are always telling young people to follow their passions. Be true to yourself. This is a vision of life that begins with self and ends with self. But people on the road to inner light do not find their vocations by asking, what do I want from life? They ask, what is life asking of me? How can I match my intrinsic talent with one of the world's deep needs?"[8]

So, what's life asking of you? What might you be ignoring? What gift would you like to leave with the world when you're gone?

HOW MY LIFE GOT BETTER ONCE I MADE ROOM FOR MY PASSIONS

These days I wake up early every morning. (Very early!)

Between the hours of 4.15am and 7am I am able to:

- Write
- Exercise
- Have time to myself where no one is talking to me or needing my attention.

Those precious morning hours play two vital roles in my life.

One, the quiet time is crucial for giving me an energy boost with which to enter the day, (introverts need time to themselves to recharge).

Two, the acts of writing and exercising allow me to nurture all of these Passions from the list I shared earlier in this section: wellness, fitness, creativity, competition, simplicity, achieving my potential, helping others achieve their potential, productivity, achievement and recognition.

Those hours also set me up for later in the day when I want to nurture my Passions for kindness and my family.

What this means is I can now weather extended periods of extreme stress (I had one that lasted for about three months just last year!) without falling into a hole. This is a big deal for someone who has spent her adult life constantly pushing through to burnout and then having to pull herself out of that hole.

Life continues to ebb and flow—but making room for my Passions has taken a distinct edge off those ebbs.

For example, in 2014 I was back working full-time in our business (yes, the same business I had to take a very long period of leave from). Trying to work full-time hours around my oldest child starting school, (those school days are *a lot* shorter than day care days), while also trying to stay on top of running our household meant I was under a huge amount of pressure. In addition, my husband was stressed out of his mind so I was trying to effectively manage my own stress levels while also buffering our kids and our staff from his.

In the past, this would have led me to burnout in no time at all. But this time, it didn't.

I was ruthless about staying in touch with some of my key Passions during those uber-stressful months, (helping people through my writing, staying fit and healthy by exercising every day and eating well). These things played a huge part in keeping me away from the deep, dark burnout hole of 'I just don't care anymore'.

They also allowed me to be clear-headed enough to activate techniques I will talk about in Sections Two and Three of this book—techniques that helped remove the extreme stress my husband and I were operating under and returned us to a more balanced state of mind.

MY CHALLENGE TO YOU

Howard Thurman once famously said:

> "Don't ask yourself what the world needs. Ask yourself what makes you come alive and then go do that. Because what the world needs is people who have come alive."

Using the thoughts and ideas shared in this section, identify just one thing you could do each day that makes you feel alive and allocate 10 minutes a day to that thing.

- 10 minutes to read up on a topic that's always interested you.

- 10 minutes to share your thoughts on something you're passionate about with your friends on Facebook.

- 10 minutes to get away from your desk at lunchtime and go for a short walk.

As you start to see the positive effect of spending just 10 minutes a day on something that lights you up inside, you will naturally start to carve out more time for it.

If you're really struggling to set aside even that 10 minutes, that means it's a good time to talk about overwhelm and its antidote, Priorities.

SECTION 2: OVERWHELM

> **Passions + Productivity in the absence of Priorities**
>
> = OVERWHELM

Another conversation with my husband.

"Kel, I'm going to be honest here. I don't see the point of therapy for you. Nothing has changed."

"What? How can you say that? It's been a huge help."

"Really? Everything looks the same from my end. You're still filling up your days with too much. You're still trying to help the world at the expense of your family. And you're still constantly stressed out, vague and distracted."

"..."

"Am I wrong?"

"No. You're not wrong. I'm sorry."

"Look, I know you're sorry. But you have to understand that your inability to find a real solution for this is very frustrating for me."

Overwhelmed people are easy to identify. They walk around in a vague and distracted manner, the stress of trying to process hundreds of things that 'have to be done right now' clearly showing on their faces. And when you ask if anything's wrong, they respond with, "I've got a lot on my mind at the moment".

As you can tell from the above conversation with my husband, 'vague and distracted' used to be my default state. I'm a naturally efficient and productive person, but throw my passions and my striver mentality into the mix and it becomes 'the perfect storm' of overwhelm: so many amazing ideas to execute, things to try 'at least once' and opportunities to grab.

So where does the overwhelm come from? From never having enough time to do all the things we want to do.

And what about the vagueness and lack of presence? That comes from constantly moving things around in our head, trying to fit it all in, despite the fact there's never enough time.

You'll know from the Practical Perfection Framework that 'fitting it all in' isn't the answer. So how else can we avoid the overwhelm, vagueness and lack of presence?

Priorities.

LET'S TALK ABOUT PRIORITIES

Here's how *Business Dictionary* defines 'prioritisation':

> As a principle, it means doing 'first things first';
> as a process, it means evaluating a group of items
> and ranking them in their order of importance or
> urgency.

Unfortunately, when you're overwhelmed *everything* seems like a priority. So how on earth do we do 'first things first' when we don't even know what the first thing should be?

In terms of the Practical Perfection Framework, Priorities come down to making good decisions about how we spend our time. But while it sounds simple enough, the reality is that few of us seem to be able to do this.

How do I know? Because the opposite of good prioritisation is overwhelm, and I see overwhelmed people everywhere. In fact, most of the emails I get from readers of my blog are from people wanting to know how to deal with overwhelm.

As part of my research for this book I conducted a survey on the topic. I wanted to know:

- Had overwhelm become the new normal?
- What were people missing out on in life because of the overwhelm?

More than 1700 people responded to my survey, with 52%

saying they felt overwhelmed either a lot or all the time. So yes, overwhelm *was* a 'normal' part of their everyday lives. And while the major *causes* of overwhelm varied greatly, the *results* of overwhelm were the same for almost everyone: increased irritability and compromised mental health.

Stop and think about what that means for a second.

If overwhelm is a normal part of people's lives, then so too are irritability and compromised mental health.

But what *really* upset me were the things people said they'd have time for if they weren't overwhelmed all the time. In my survey I asked them to finish this sentence: "When I'm not feeling stressed out and overwhelmed I have more time for ...". And here's a *very* indicative sample of their responses:

> "*Pursuing creative activities like singing, playing, recording, drawing and cooking.*"

> "*Fun, frivolity and spontaneity. More time to be the person I like being.*"

> "*Having fun and being in the moment with my kids and husband - laughing, being silly and wasting time.*"

> "*Just breathing, and just being.*"

> "*Being a giver: a giver of my time, my listening, my support and my love. If I am in my happy place I have abundantly more capacity to give.*"

It was heartbreaking to see what people were missing out on (and *knew* they were missing out on) because they couldn't get on top of their Priorities. It was doubly heartbreaking to realise they didn't feel they had the tools or the capacity to change the situation.

To understand how we got to this point, we first need to know one key thing about overwhelm.

OVERWHELM IS A VERY BAD HABIT

At the core of every habit (good or bad) is a simple three-part loop:

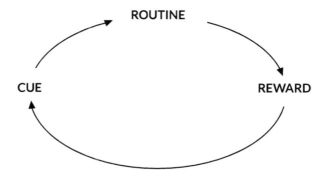

The cue triggers a routine/action that ultimately leads to a reward. Habits that are highly automated (and extremely hard to break) are those where your brain anticipates the pleasure of the upcoming reward the moment it 'sees' the cue.

For example:

> Right on **cue** at 3pm, you hit a bit of a slump. This triggers the **routine** of heading over to the coffee shop, where you **reward** yourself with a coffee and 'something sweet' for making it this far through the day. After doing it for months it becomes such a strong habit that seeing '3pm' on your watch is enough to make the pleasure centres in your brain light up at the thought of how good that coffee and 'something sweet' will taste.
>
> It's that **craving** that causes the habit to become very automated.

If you love helping other people (like I do), a similar scenario plays out when someone asks you to do something for them:

> Your friend Annie comes past your desk at work and says:
>
> *"I've been asked to stay back to help with that big tender we're working on. But I've got no one to pick up Sally from school..."*
>
> You say:
>
> *"Oh gosh, no dramas. I can pick Sally up for you and take her back to my place. Come through and grab her once you're finished up here."*

What's the reward here? Your friend's relief and gratitude, and the genuine dopamine hit that comes with that.

Now, there's nothing inherently wrong with this scenario. After all, friends helping friends is what makes the world go round. The problems start when you become addicted to the dopamine hit that grateful face delivers. You soon realise *anyone* asking for help can give you that hit, and you find yourself saying "Yes" in your head before they've even asked their favour. Before you know it, you're not only helping your friend Annie but everyone else who asks for help as well.

This is exactly what happened to me. (You can probably understand my husband's frustration now.)

Now, if all we needed to do is break the overwhelm habit loop, Prioritising would be relatively easy to do. But a few other things can also cause overwhelm for those wanting to live an excellent life.

WHAT ELSE DRIVES OVERWHELM?

Cause of overwhelm #1:
Needing to use up every available minute of the day

This one usually rears its head when your Passions are in full flight. If you're anything like me, you have so many ideas that most of them are sitting on the sidelines, waiting to be brought into play. Still, you have enough common sense to know that while you've always been able to do *a lot*, you can't do *everything*.

But then some free time becomes available to you, and I'll bet my house the resulting conversation in your head goes something like this:

Wait—is that a tiny opening in my schedule I see? Unreal! This is my chance to finally do project x, which has been hovering on the edge of my mind for ages. I've been so good at not giving in to its seductive siren call, so it would be a crime not to do it given I can't stop thinking about it right?

Maybe.

But when you think about it, probably not.

Cause of overwhelm #2:
FODO—Fear Of Disappointing Others

I've already touched on FODO in terms of being asked to do something and not being able to say no. But the strivers' need to rise to other people's expectations (whether they're reasonable or not) can also cause problems.

I've had emails from people who, because of FODO:

- Spent 30 years in a career they found incredibly unfulfilling.

- Found themselves on a time-consuming fundraising committee because they had a tenuous link to what the funds were for and the committee assumed they'd be up for it.

- Wound up horribly in debt and struggling to pay it off because their friends went on a trip to Europe and expected them to come too.

The problem with FODO is it becomes self-perpetuating. The more we do for people, and the more we rise to meet their expectations, the more they expect from us. And the more they expect from us, the less we want to 'disappoint' them by saying no.

Cause of overwhelm #3:
FOMO—Fear Of Missing Out

In 2013 the term 'FOMO' was added to the Oxford English Dictionary. And while the fear of missing out on something cool has always been part of the human make-up, social media has ramped it up to unbelievable levels.

Wikipedia defines FOMO as:

"*A pervasive apprehension that others might be having rewarding experiences from which one is absent. This social angst is characterized by a desire to stay continually connected with what others are doing. FOMO is also defined as a fear of regret, which may lead to a compulsive concern that one might miss an opportunity for social interaction, a novel experience, profitable investment or other satisfying event. In other words, FOMO perpetuates the fear of having made the wrong decision on how to spend time, as you can imagine how things could be different.*"[9]

That last sentence is why social media, an ever-present part of lives today, is sending FOMO into the stratosphere. Before the Internet, we needed to actually *see* people doing cool things (or hear about it after the fact) to imagine how things could be different. But thanks to social media we can now see everything we *could* be doing—all in real time—and we're changing our behaviour as a result.

We see people out together, wonder why we weren't invited, and start spending time doing things to ensure we *are* invited next time.

After seeing peers achieving something that's on our bucket list, (but somewhere near the bottom), we suddenly feel compelled to have a crack at it sooner rather than later.

Worst of all, social media can make us feel we *should* be doing activities or striving for goals that, deep down, we know aren't for us.

For example, despite being highly driven my whole life I've never wanted to do stuff on a global scale. But seeing what my female entrepreneur friends are up to sometimes makes me think I'm aiming too low, and that what I *am* doing isn't enough.

Bringing the word 'should' into the mix is always dangerous. Why? Because it indicates both a lack of self-awareness (of what's realistic for ourselves) and self-acceptance (we're judging ourselves by what we've *not* accomplished rather than by what we have).

So, what's the first step to getting a better grip on reality and bringing greater self-acceptance into the mix in order to prioritise better?

We need to get in touch with our values.

LET'S TALK ABOUT VALUES

What are values exactly?

They are:

> " ... *those elements of your life which you find personally important. They are core beliefs which guide you on how to conduct your life in a way that is meaningful and satisfying for you.*
>
> *Values are the things against which you measure your choices, whether consciously or not. You use them to rationalise your behaviour to yourself and others. And they determine your level of satisfaction with your choices, even if decisions are not freely made but constrained by other factors.*"[10]

What do values have to do with Priorities?

Roy E. Disney has been credited with saying:

> "*It's not hard to make decisions when you know what your values are.*"

Given that making (good) decisions is what effective prioritisation is all about, it's really important to understand what your values are before trying to prioritise your time effectively.

So how do you figure out what your values are?

As well as conducting considerable research on the topic, I asked several well-qualified people for their answers to that particular question. In the end, psychologist Ellen Jackson summed up my findings really well:

> "Values is actually a really under-researched area in psychology."

Translation: there's no sure-fire way to truly understand what your values are.

Ellen went on to say the simplest and most often used tool is a values inventory. And she has generously provided the values inventory she uses in her *Find Your Groove* course, which you can find (along with some introductory prompts) in Appendix 1.

Equally generous was Lee Alexander from Brightside Coaching, who provided the Core Values Exercise she uses in her program *The Flourish Project*®. You can find that in Appendix 2.

Meanwhile, here's an exercise I've walked people through on my website that incorporates elements of both the above. It involves three sets of questions:

1: Describe a (hopefully recent) situation where you felt super 'buzzy'/energised/on top of your game.

- Where were you, who were you with, and what were you doing?
- How did you come to be there?
- What was it about the situation that made you feel so buzzy/energised?

2: Describe a (hopefully recent) situation or moment where you felt ridiculously content.

- Where were you, who were you with, and what were you doing?
- How did you come to be there?
- What was it about the situation that made you feel so content?

3: Quick analysis

- Looking at your answers, what jumps out as something that you value highly or brings out the best in you?

Because I know it's always helpful to see these things in action, here are my answers to the above:

1: Describe a (hopefully recent) situation where you felt super 'buzzy'/energised/on top of your game.

Where were you? A conference.

What were you doing? Speaking!

Who were you with? A large group of peers.

How did you come to be there? I put in an application to speak four years in a row, and finally got a YES!

What was it about the situation that made you feel so buzzy/energised? I was speaking (because I love speaking/presenting) to a group of my peers (i.e. people who already 'got' what I was going to be talking about). There was also the validation of being chosen to speak, and the lovely feedback I received afterwards. I was on a high for a week after the event.

2: Describe a (hopefully recent) situation or moment where you felt ridiculously content.

Where were you? At home in our backyard.

What were you doing? Chatting to my husband (Ant) and kicking a footy around with the kids.

Who were you with? Ant and the kids.

How did you come to be there? Ant and I have worked quite hard to be in a position where we can both be home in the afternoon to enjoy some quality time with the kids each day.

What was it about the situation that made you feel so content? Everyone was so chilled out. The kids were stoked to be out in the backyard with both their parents. And Ant and I were feeling (at the time) very un-stressed, so we could have a nice conversation without any angsty-ness! It was so nice being able to be fully present with my family and enjoying time with them without any tension or distractedness because of worries and stresses!

Part 3: Quick analysis

Going on your answers to the above, what is jumping out at you as things you value highly/bring out the best in you?

Recognition from my peers. Being able to help people by sharing my knowledge. Quality time with my family. Being fully present and 'in the moment' with my family.

The good thing about these questions is that whenever you're in a situation that makes you feel ridiculously buzzy or content you can run through the 'sub' questions, hone in on *why* the situation is making you buzzy, and translate that knowledge into a value.

If the questions *haven't* sparked anything for you, please check out the resources Ellen and Lee have provided. When it comes to values, sometimes you just need to come at things from a slightly different direction to achieve that real 'Aha!' moment. And let me assure you it's definitely worth the effort, as you'll now see.

HOW DO VALUES DRIVE GOOD DECISION MAKING?

Let me share my own experience.

As I've mentioned, it's easy for someone who's highly driven like me to look at peers, (entrepreneurs and writers with young families), doing massive things on the world stage and think, "If they can manage to do those things, then I should try to do them too". (There's that word 'should' again.)

Then I remember that one of my absolute core values is the need to *be at home*. I could never travel as much as they do because I get terribly (and I mean *terribly*) homesick.

Note: This value is separate from the strong values I have around 'family'. My successful, world-dominating female friends have strong family values too. But they don't have that deep-seated need to *be at home* like I do.

Some of my core values are slightly contradictory, and I have to find a way for them to work together. For example, my core values of *achievement* and *recognition* have the potential to clash rather badly with the values I have around *privacy* and *space*.

I've come to understand that the best way for them to work together was to aim for recognition only from my peers. (In other words, to never be so 'famous' that random people recognise me on the street.)

Knowing all of this means I can check myself whenever cool opportunities present themselves:

- Will this thing regularly prevent me from being at home in the evenings or on the weekends? If so, then the answer will probably be "No".

- Will this thing give me wider exposure than I'm comfortable with? If so, then the answer will probably be "No".

- Will it put me in the position of losing much-valued privacy and space? If so, then the answer will probably be "No" (no matter how much my ego is screaming "Do it! Do it!").

EIGHT PRACTICAL TIPS FOR TACKLING OVERWHELM

Now that you have a better understanding of what your values are, and feel more capable of making good decisions about what your Priorities really are, here are eight other mindset shifts to help you keep a lid on overwhelm.

Tackle overwhelm #1:
Don't compare someone's highlight reel
with your everyday life

Social media is great for showing us the highlights of people's lives. But it rarely shows us what happens behind the curtain.

- The friend currently at a resort in Bali isn't Instagramming herself stressed out in her hotel room trying to make a tight deadline.

- The colleague who won that award isn't telling you how the ridiculously long hours they worked in the past year affected their relationship with their partner and kids.

- Your brother might have just moved into a beautiful new house, but he's not sharing how he can't actually afford the mortgage.

- The mum at school who lost all that weight isn't confessing it was all due to the stress of her marriage failing.

As much as we keep hearing it, we can't help being envious of the nice things we see other people experiencing. But it's really important to remember we don't know the story behind the highlight reel. And the best way to remind ourselves of this is by noting what *we* aren't telling people next time we share something cool on social media.

Tackle overwhelm #2:
Understand that no one has it 'all'

In the same vein, somewhere along the line we decided there are actually people out there who:

Are training for an Ironman triathlon, while going on holiday to The Maldives, while maintaining a house that looks like a magazine, while making Nigella-style dinners every night, while attending their kids' award assembly, while running a fundraiser for their friend who's got cancer, while winning a much-coveted business award, while having a weekly date night with their partner.

Yep, we cherry-pick the best parts of everyone's lives on Facebook or Instagram, put them together to create an awesome life absolutely no-one is living, and label it 'having it all'.

Crazy, right? But we all do it—even the most self-aware of us.

Overcoming this is as simple as catching ourselves doing it, and then reminding ourselves that 'having it all' is nothing more than a fantasy.

Tackle overwhelm #3:
Understand that other people's goals
are not your goals

As a writer, I have a lot of writer friends. (It goes with the territory.) For many of them, their big goal is to have a publisher come and tell them, "I love your book and I want to publish it". So it would be easy for me to think it should be my goal as well.

The thing is, while I'd love to see my book sitting face out in an airport bookstore I know I'd struggle with the traditional publishing process: the long lead times, the need to get the manuscript past several gatekeepers, the loss of creative control. I love the nimbleness of self-publishing—getting my words into the hands of readers as quickly as possible while having complete control over my own destiny.

It's *really* important to know that just because your peers have an aspiration to achieve something, this doesn't mean *you* should have the same aspiration.

It can be a hard thing to push back against sometimes (okay, a lot of the time). But when you make decisions based on your values instead of what everyone else is doing (or suggesting you should do), the feeling of relief will tell you everything you need to know.

Tackle overwhelm #4:
Understand that your Priorities
may not be Priorities at all

The other day I felt a pang of jealousy towards a friend who had an article published on a site I've long dreamed of being published on. But it quickly faded when I realised that even though I dreamed of being published there, I hadn't:

- Followed the site in more than a cursory manner.

- Taken note of the types of things they've published.

- Built any kind of relationship with the people who run the site.

- Ever actually submitted a piece to them for publication.

Getting published on that site clearly wasn't as big a priority as I thought it was, or I would have been a little more proactive about it. Right?

Tackle overwhelm #5:
Get comfortable with disappointing others

In 2012 my guiding word for the year was 'No'. After battling extreme overwhelm for my entire adult life, I decided it was time to stop pleasing people and get comfortable with FODO.

What I was most scared about: People feeling let down and being upset with me when I said 'No' to them.

What actually happened: People felt let down and became upset with me when I said 'No' to them. And then ... they got over it really quickly.

As an added bonus, the whole process gave people a better understanding of my boundaries. I was asked to do things less often, which meant I didn't have to say 'No' as much. Win!

Tackle overwhelm #6:
Understand the 'sunk cost' fallacy

One of the biggest enemies of getting on top of overwhelm is 'sunk costs'. When we've invested a lot of time and effort into something, we just can't bear the thought of 'losing out' on that investment by walking away from it.

This is true of:

- The person who started an online shop and invested time and money creating products.

- Athletes who've made huge sacrifices and spent years training for a particular event.

- People who've paid a significant deposit towards an overseas conference.

We need to understand that while we may be losing significant 'sunk costs' by walking away from something, continuing to pursue it may end up costing us a lot more. I'm not saying we should all just throw in the towel when the going gets tough. But if your gut is telling you loud and clear that it's time to walk away, give yourself permission to listen.

Tackle overwhelm #7:
Make peace with your striver personality

For people who hold themselves to high standards and are clear about what their Passions are in life, the sky's the limit! Unfortunately, the resources available to us (time, energy, space) are not. So we have to accept that:

- We can't go after everything that presents itself to us.

- Sometimes things will happen more slowly than we'd like.

- Sometimes we'll miss out on things because we weren't in the right place at the right time.

This is where knowing our values comes in handy. They reaffirm the things we're spending time and energy on are truly important to us, and allow us to be more realistic in what we expect both of ourselves and life in general.

Tackle overwhelm #8:
Learn six simple words

Originally this book was going to be called *How to Say No*—specifically, 'How to say no to overwhelm'. But I ran into a bit of trouble when I realised everything I wanted to tell people about learning to say no came down to six simple words: '*Let me get back to you.*'

Those six words are what got me through 2012, the 'Year of Saying No' I mentioned earlier.

They helped me override the very bad 'saying yes to everything and everyone and horribly over-committing myself on an ongoing basis' habit I mentioned at the beginning of this section.

They allowed me to go away, check in with my values, get a good feel for what I was really saying yes to, and *then* give the person an answer. They also let whoever made the request know that 'No' was a possibility before I said it (if that was my answer).

And even if the answer *was* 'No', I rarely said it. Instead I'd use some variation of:

- Thank you so much for the opportunity, but it isn't right for me at the moment.
- I can't help you with that at the moment, but perhaps you could try x.
- I wish I could be involved, but the current constraints on my time don't allow for it.

HOW MY LIFE GOT BETTER ONCE I IDENTIFIED MY PRIORITIES

Like most people reading this book, overwhelm has been an ever-present companion in my life. As an 'achiever', I've always found it hard to say no to anything resembling an 'opportunity'. And as someone who loves to help people, I've always found it hard to say no to requests for help.

I'd always known that one of my core values was to be more present when with my family—yet I was failing to Prioritise that in my rush to be everywhere, do everything and ensure I never missed an opportunity.

It's taken long, hard conversations with my husband to remind me that when I said 'yes' to certain things, I was saying 'no' to something else. And that 'something else' was usually him, our kids, or both.

These days, whenever I find myself getting overwhelmed, I do two things:

1. I try not to beat myself up for finding myself in an overwhelmed state again.

2. I remind myself what my true Priorities are, and then make the necessary adjustments to get back to where I want to be.

As an example, towards the end of 2015 I felt like I was drowning in life. Given I was also in the middle of finishing this book at the time, I felt so stupid. Was it appropriate for someone who was writing about overwhelm to find themselves in an overwhelmed state?

It was important to recognise that berating myself for feeling overwhelmed wasn't really helping anything. It was only once I was able to move past that feeling that I was able to do something useful—figure out which of the things I was overwhelmed by were true Priorities … and get rid of the rest.

This is what I love about the Practical Perfection Framework. It doesn't judge me for having strayed from the centre zone. It just reminds me what I need to do to get back there.

MY CHALLENGE TO YOU

The one thing that has helped me stay on top of overwhelm more than any other has been the ability to utter the phrase:

"Let me get back to you."

So if there is just one thing I'd love you to try for the next few weeks, it's that. Whenever someone asks you to do something, or offers you an opportunity, do not say 'Yes' straight away. Get back to them.

You might get back to them in 30 seconds (say if it's your child asking for a piece of cake), or you might get back to them the next day (in the case of someone asking you to be involved in a project). Just remove the knee-jerk 'Yes' from your repertoire for a few weeks and see what kind of effect it has on your overall overwhelm levels.

Now let's move on to the final piece of the Practical Perfection puzzle—Productivity.

SECTION 3:
HAMSTER ON A WHEEL

> **Priorities + Passions in the absence of Productivity**
> = HAMSTER ON A WHEEL

Yet another conversation with my husband.

"Ant, I need you to register a domain name for me."

"Another one? What's this one for?"

"Just an idea I've got."

"Another idea ..."

"What?"

"It's just that you're supposed to be at home getting better, but instead you're chasing after every single idea that enters your head. You're busy, busy, busy, just like you've always been. But it just doesn't seem like you're actually getting anywhere."

We've all met that person who seems to have a 'great new idea' every time you speak to them. You get really excited for them, and can't wait for an update next time you see them. But when you do, they've already moved on to something else they're just as passionate about. Again, you get really excited for them, and look forward to hearing more. But sure enough, the next time you see them they've moved on again.

Eventually you stop getting excited about their ideas because you realise they never actually make them happen.

For some people, this is their default setting. They're 'ideas' people who need 'doers' to take their ideas and make them a reality.

But when strivers (people who are generally good at Making Things Happen) fall into this pattern of behaviour, it's usually because (to borrow a phrase from Zig Ziglar) they've started confusing activity with accomplishment.

When I had my breakdown and my husband sent me home to get better while he took over running my business, I was completely lost.

I felt guilty for being at home doing 'nothing' instead of contributing to the household budget. I felt completely rudderless because 'getting better' was a pretty vague thing to be working towards. And I felt extremely agitated because I wasn't achieving anything.

So I did what I always do when I feel a bit 'lost' in life: I got busy. I signed up for courses, took on passion projects and, worst of all, started new businesses.

It wasn't long before I was, once again, the proverbial hamster on a wheel.

LET'S TALK ABOUT PRODUCTIVITY

Most people think of Productivity as the ability to fit more into the available hours of their day. And I certainly used to leverage Productivity in this manner. As you know from Section One, when I had my first baby I managed to fit an insane amount of stuff into my days. But all that netted me was burnout.

These days? As counter-intuitive as it may seem, I use Productivity to create time in my day for what I call 'meandering'.

The short story of meandering is this: if you build pockets of time into your days where you have more time than you need to get things done, you're better placed to cope with the 'surprises' life likes to throw at all of us. We all know how reactive and out of control we feel when our days are scheduled down to the last minute. Making time to meander reduces that reactiveness greatly.

So how do we introduce more Productivity into our lives in a way that allows us to make more time to meander?

Well, it's a four-step process:

1. Get your focus right.

2. Get your energy levels right.

3. Create whitespace.

4. Get stuff done.

GET PRODUCTIVE STEP 1:
GET YOUR FOCUS RIGHT

My clever friend Nicole Avery once said:

> "If you're spending your time on the wrong activities, no matter how well you manage your time, you won't be productive."[11]

When we're in tune with our Passions, and our Priorities are in place so we have time to nurture those Passions, every idea seems great and worthy of our time. So we have a crack at everything that catches our eye. Here's what this looks like:

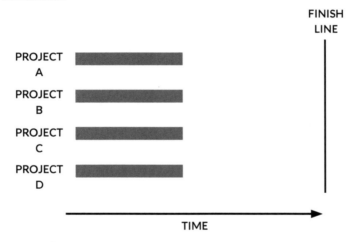

Yep, we're really busy. And we're certainly 'doing' a lot. But because we're not actually finishing anything, we're not really getting anywhere.

And if you've ever been in this situation, you'll know how demotivating it is.

Here's what happens when we focus that same amount of time on fewer projects:

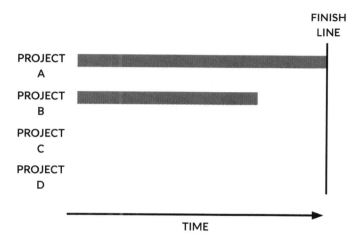

Project A is done. Project B is nearly finished. And Projects C and D are still there, waiting their turn.

So before we can get Productive in a way that removes that hamster-on-a-wheel feeling, we need to narrow our focus. It doesn't mean we have to limit our Passions, or take on fewer projects. We just need to understand that to actually get somewhere, we need to tackle one thing at a time.

And I get it. I really do. When you're a striver, there are so many things you could be doing. It can be really hard to maintain focus, but it's so rewarding when you do.

Once you've zeroed in on what you want to achieve, the next step in the Productivity process is getting your energy levels right.

GET PRODUCTIVE STEP 2: GET YOUR ENERGY LEVELS RIGHT

It's been said that while you can't change the number of hours you have in a day, you *can* change the amount of energy you bring to those hours.

I couldn't agree more. So many people think burning the candle at both ends makes them incredibly productive, but all it really does is put them on a fast path to burnout.

Here are three key foundations to having the right energy levels:

Energy levels foundation 1: Exercise

Too many people look at exercise as just a weight loss tool. They believe if they don't need to lose weight (or weight loss isn't a priority for them), then they don't need to exercise.

The fact is, our bodies are designed to move. Unless we're moving, our bodies aren't operating at optimal capacity. Exercise is essential for good mental health and, as counter-intuitive as it seems, also boosts energy levels.

But that doesn't necessarily mean hitting the gym or training for a marathon. Something as simple as a 30-minute walk each day is enough to give us the energy boost we need.

When should you exercise? Whenever you can fit it in. Morning exercisers love how it kicks off their day, to the point where they feel mentally sluggish if they *don't* get their morning exercise. Midday exercisers love how it gives their brains a rest in the middle of the day and boosts their afternoon productivity. And afternoon/evening exercisers love how it dissipates the stresses of their day and helps them sleep better.

Figure out what works best for you, and then commit to it.

Energy levels foundation 2: Sleep

Sleep is often the first thing that goes out the window when you're flat to the ground trying to meet the standards you've set for yourself.

While it's generally accepted that adults need eight to nine hours of sleep at night to function well, I don't necessarily agree with that. Mainly because I only need seven. So I'm more with Hal Elrod (author of *Miracle Morning*), who thinks each individual needs a different amount of sleep to function well and we all just need to figure out what that amount is. Then we need to make sure we don't just get those hours, but that they are *quality* hours.

Unfortunately, it's that quality that most of us struggle with—especially if we have kids.

The ironic thing is, we all *know* how important sleep is, and how unproductive we are without it—fuelling our bodies with coffee and holding our eyes open with matchsticks just to get through the day. Yet we keep staying up really late, or worse, going to bed on time but taking our phones to bed and spending an hour scrolling through Instagram. I won't say getting quality sleep is easy, but we certainly do a lot to sabotage our chances.

Some simple tips for getting good sleep:

1. Go to bed at the same time each night. (Our bodies like routine and rhythm.)

2. Go to bed at a decent hour. My favourite 'tool' for this is to have a great book I'm really looking forward to reading.

3. No screens an hour before bedtime. (I head to bed with my great book an hour before my ideal time to fall asleep.)

4. No electronics in the bedroom. (Studies have shown they interrupt our sleep.)

5. Exercise every day.

6. Before you head off to bed, write down your 'must dos' for the following day. Knowing exactly what's in store will help your mind relax.

7. Eat dinner at least two (preferably three) hours before bedtime.

8. Have a notepad next to your bed so anything that wakes you up at 3am can be quickly written down and then 'forgotten' about.

Energy levels foundation 3: Food

Another key component of energy is food—something else we ignore when under the pump. Mind you, food seems to have become really complicated lately. Should you go Paleo, Whole30, no sugar, vegan, vegetarian ... pegan?

The truth is, we all know how to eat healthily: choose food that's made from scratch over packaged and processed food as much as possible, stick to eating food we've prepared ourselves, and control our portion sizes.

Don't have time? Don't like cooking? That's okay. Neither do I, which is why I keep things *really* simple.

For me, the hardest thing about moving from packaged food (the diet I used to have) to cooking my own food (my diet now) has always been that first attempt at making something. It takes time (and sometimes a few attempts) to learn a new recipe. But once I know how to cook something, I become very efficient at it.

For example, I can make a spinach and roast pumpkin salad from scratch in about ten minutes these days—five if I am organised enough to roast the pumpkin the day before. It sure beats warming up a meat pie for lunch.

While we're on the topic of lunch, if you're busy you may be tempted to grab something quick and easy and then eat it while working at your desk to stay productive. I used to do the same thing.

But then I forced myself to step away from my desk and all those screens at lunchtime, and eat my lunch while reading the paper or sitting on the verandah in the sun. And my afternoon Productivity skyrocketed.

Don't think you have time to do the same? Fifteen minutes is all you need. And we all have 15 minutes for lunch—trust me.

GET PRODUCTIVE STEP 3: CREATE WHITESPACE

As I mentioned earlier in this section, many people see Productivity as a tool that lets us fit more into our days. But thinking this way can lead to what I call the Trap of Productivity:

> *The more productive we are, the more we can do. But the more we do, the more productive we need to be.*

Once we get caught in this dangerous cycle, we have to become insanely productive *every single day* just to get through everything we've signed ourselves up for. And with each day scheduled down to the minute, the tiniest thing can completely derail it:

- A narky email from a client that needs a detailed answer.

- An unexpected phone call from a friend.

- The doctor who's running behind even though you're their first appointment.

- The slow driver you're stuck behind.

- The toddler who does a poo just as you finish buckling them into their car seat.

Suddenly we're reacting to these normal, everyday events with frustration, anger, and declarations about everybody wasting our time.

I don't know about you, but feeling frustrated and angry all the time kind of messes with my life of Practical Perfection.

That's why I use Productivity to create whitespace instead.

What's whitespace?

Whitespace is actually a graphic design element that:

- Lets the other elements on the page breathe.

- Reduces tension between elements.

- Lets the most important things come to the fore.

- Is essential for balance and harmony in a design.

And if that's what whitespace can do for a design, imagine what it can do for a person.

Actually, you don't have to. Let me tell you a story about what it did for me.

It was one of those days at the bank. The line was long and slow-moving—every person in front of me seemed to have long and complicated transactions. By the time a teller became available for my own long and complicated transaction I'd already been waiting in line for 20 minutes.

The teller smiled at me apologetically and got to work. Twenty minutes later it was finally done.

As she stacked and stapled my paperwork and handed it to me she offered a profuse apology. "Thanks so much for your patience," she said. "I know you don't have time for this."

I smiled back at her. "It's all good."

And as I spoke I experienced a revelation. I *did* have time for this.

There was a time when I would have stood in line checking my watch overtly, tapping my feet and sighing. I probably would have even dreamt of sending the bank an invoice for Wasting My Time because time is money, right?

But not that day. That day I had time to 'waste' standing around in the bank for 20 minutes longer than expected.

And it felt great.

It felt great not to be angry and fuming. It felt great being able to reassure the harried teller it was all okay. It felt great to get in my car without having to rush to my next destination feeling harassed and dangerously distracted.

Think of all the times someone has 'wasted your time' or 'messed with your plans'. Now think about how you reacted to those people (anger, frustration, making them feel bad about themselves). Can you see how the positive effects of whitespace extend way beyond just you?

How do you get more whitespace in your life?

To begin with you need to stop scheduling your days down to the minute. You need to create pockets of time in your day where you can move slowly (be able to 'meander') and have plenty of time for what needs to be done.

For me, between 7am and 8.15am is one of those pockets of time. All I have to do in that hour and a bit is get my toddler up and dressed, make a green smoothie for myself and my husband, and clean up everyone's breakfast dishes.

I could fit a *lot* more into that time if I wanted to. I could put a load of laundry on. I could prep dinner. I could check and answer emails.

But I don't.

That chilled out hour or so in the morning means I'm not yelling at the kids because we're running late. It means that if one of the kids spills milk all over the floor, or announces they need to study for a spelling test, it doesn't derail the entire morning (and the rest of the day). It means I get to walk out the front door feeling chilled and ready to take on the day instead of frustrated and flustered. (I've found that if you start your day frustrated and flustered it's very hard to pull things back from there.)

What else helps with whitespace? Having a routine.

The importance of routine

Every productive person you will ever come across believes in routine. Hand on my heart, I haven't yet met one who has found 'flying by the seat of their pants' to be an effective way to go about things.

That's because having a routine reduces cognitive load. The more stuff you can do on autopilot, the more room you have for ideas and making stuff happen.

Having a routine also minimises potential problems and curveballs, reducing the need to react to unexpected events (which in turn reduces stress).

Finally, routine is crucial for Productivity because it lets you despatch frequently done tasks more quickly and efficiently.

Ironically, routine also lets you create space in your day for spontaneity, and reduces the need to call on willpower and motivation.

So how do you go about building routines into your days?

Remember: you're not creating a routine *for* your day. You're adding routines *to* your day.

As an example, here's the routine I follow in the morning:

My morning routine

4.15am: *Wake up, drink two big glasses of water while browsing Instagram and making a coffee.*

4:30am: *Quickly scan emails and delete the crap.*

4:45am: *Write for 45 minutes to an hour.*

5:30am-ish: *Do morning exercise (running, rowing, walking or CrossFit).*

6:30am: *Get home from exercise, make my six-year-old's school lunch.*

7am: *Get toddler up and enjoy morning cuddles with her on the couch before making a breakfast smoothie for myself and my husband.*

7:30am: *Tidy up kitchen, have a shower and get dressed.*

8:15am: *Do school drop-off with my son.*

Here's why my morning routine is so important:

- It ensures I get time for myself every day.

- It ensures I get time to write every day. My energy levels for writing are highest in the morning when no-one else is around or wants to talk to me, so that's when I do it.

- It ensures I do some form of exercise every day. (Hopefully I've sold you on the importance of daily exercise.)

- It ensures that I'm in a good mood when the rest of my family wakes up so I can deal with any of *their* grumpiness with good humour.

- It ensures our mornings are chilled, which means we're all calm when we walk out the door to start our days. (Remember: the way you leave the house in the morning has a huge effect on how the rest of your day pans out.)

- It gives my brain a break. Instead of spending those hours trying to figure out what I should do next, I'm operating pretty much on autopilot.

My morning routine is important. But I also have other routines I follow throughout the day.

For example, embedded in that morning routine is both a **writing routine** and an **exercise routine**. Having these two routines means I don't have to waste willpower trying to motivate myself to write or exercise. I just do them.

You'll notice I also have the same thing for breakfast every morning (green smoothie). Not having to decide what to have for breakfast every morning has freed up an incredible amount of mental space.

We also have an **afternoon routine** in our house that starts when I get home from the afternoon school run and finishes with me putting dinner on the table.

Then we have an **evening routine** that revolves around the kids having baths and then us chilling out as a family before the kids go to bed. (Yes, we even schedule 'chill out' time into our evenings.)

Once the kids are in bed I have a **'get ready for the next day' routine** that makes me feel on top of the next day and thus helps me sleep better.

On the weekends I have a Sunday afternoon **'get ready for the next week' routine** that's all about feeling on top of the week ahead.

One of the biggest advantages I find with these routines is that they eliminate most surprises. I don't find out at 8am that there's no bread in the fridge to make my son's school lunch, or head off to get dressed in the morning only to discover I have no clean clothes.

They also lower the chance of surprises for the rest of my family. Ever had to tell your partner they have 30 minutes to conjure up a Book Week costume? Or that they have to do the morning drop off at school because you forgot about your early appointment? If you have, you'll know it leads to both an ugly reaction and a lot of unnecessary stress.

By having routines you can identify anything that's *out of routine* much earlier, and notify anyone it affects *before* it becomes an issue.

So how do you create a routine?

Well, first you need to know your desired outcome.

- The desired outcome of my morning routine is that instead of our mornings being full of angst and people yelling at each other because, "I can't believe you don't have your shoes on yet", we can all walk out of the house and head off to school, day care and work feeling chilled and ready for the day.

- The desired outcome of my writing routine is to ensure I write at least 750 words every day.

- The desired outcome of my exercise routine is to ensure I move my body for at least 20 minutes every day.

- The desired outcome of my afternoon routine is to set things up for the evening routine.

- The desired outcome of my evening routine is for us all to have some quality time together as a family.

- The desired outcome of my 'get ready for the next day' routine is to feel on top of the next day so I sleep well that night.

Once you know the desired outcome, you can create the steps necessary to achieve it. For example, the steps involved in my **'get ready for the next day' routine** are:

1. Checking my diary to see what's on.

2. Putting out my exercise clothes for the next morning, along with the clothes I'll be wearing for the day.

3. Moving the meat for dinner the following evening from the freezer to the fridge.

4. Doing a final tidy to ensure I can lay down on the couch to chill out before bed without feeling agitated by seeing mess out of the corner of my eye, and that I can wake up the next morning without being faced with dishes in the sink.

The most important thing with any routine is being able to repeat it over and over again. If you're struggling to execute a given routine then either you're trying to fit too much into the time you've allocated or your energy levels are too low.

And the best thing about routines? When 'things happen' that derail your entire day, it's not a problem because you get to start again fresh the following day. And your routines provide a way to 'reset' rather than feeling you're starting from scratch.

How do routines create whitespace?

As I mentioned earlier, routines create *mental* whitespace by reducing cognitive load. But they also create *literal* whitespace, because when you execute a routine day after day you become more efficient.

The key here is to avoid using your newfound efficiency to fit more stuff in. Allow yourself to use the space you've created to move more slowly, or to do 'time wasting' but fun things such as messing around on Facebook or Instagram.

The ability to move slowly is often seen as a luxury reserved for holidays. A key goal of the Practical Perfection Framework is to feel like you have that luxury every day.

GET PRODUCTIVE STEP 4: GET STUFF DONE

So you've created routines in your life to give you some whitespace, and you've made some time to meander. But there are times during the day when you need to be uber-productive. How do you ensure you're getting the most out of those times?

Here are eight practical tips to elevate your Productivity:

Get stuff done tip 1:
Know what needs to be done

Sounds silly and simplistic, right? But how often have you sat down at your computer and thought, "Hmm. What do I need to get done today?" or "Where should I start?"

I never sit down at my computer without knowing what I'm going to do. Otherwise I can pretty much guarantee I'll open a browser window and click on Facebook.

Now, I'm not going to get into the nitty gritty of how to make a to-do list here. Everyone has a preference about how to do it, and I'm certainly not going to claim my way is the best way.

But I will say this: Your to-do list should be *doable*.

Don't make it so long that half of the items wind up on the following day's list. Make a list you can actually complete.

The 'must dos' should be at the top, followed by the 'nice to dos'.

It should allow for unforeseen events—the nasty email you need to answer carefully, the half-hour conversation with a friend who calls out of the blue, or that long queue at the bank.

It should also group similar items together. If you have to pay three bills, pay them all at the same time. If you have five emails to answer, set aside thirty minutes and do them all in one hit.

Ok, maybe I *am* going to tell you how to make a to-do list!

Get stuff done tip 2:
Reduce the time available to do things

You've heard the adage that the time it takes to do something will expand to fill the time allocated for it, right? Well, it's true. If you have four hours to get a report done, then you'll use every one of those hours to do it. But if you only have an hour to get it done, you'll get it done in an hour.

Will the report you spent four hours writing be any better? In most cases, no.

My favourite way of reducing the time available for things is to mandate a five-hour work day for myself. My husband and I run a design business together, and while it would be easy to be jealous of his 8.30am-5pm work day, I can accomplish a surprising amount in my 9.30am-2.30pm work day.

Here's why. When you have a five-hour work day you don't go on Facebook 'just for five minutes', write a 500-word reply to someone's forum post or spend 20 minutes making a coffee. You get to your desk knowing exactly what needs to be done and then you get busy doing it.

Get stuff done tip 3:
Know the difference between urgent and important

I'm sure you've seen the Eisenhower Decision Matrix. (If you haven't, here it is.)

	URGENT	NOT URGENT
IMPORTANT	Urgent and important	Important but not urgent
NOT IMPORTANT	Urgent but not important	Not urgent and not important

Where do we all tend to spend most of our time? In the **Urgent and Important** and **Urgent but Not Important** quadrants.

That **Urgent but Not Important** quadrant is a major Productivity killer. It involves things like responding to emails (which are usually driven by other people's priorities, not ours), putting out fires, and generally being reactive. When you're always operating in this quadrant it's almost impossible to get anything truly useful done.

The **Important but Not Urgent** quadrant is all about our mental and physical wellbeing. It's where those things that make us nicer people tend to reside—exercise, business development, dreaming, reading, relaxing, etc. But all too often we have to put those things aside because we're too busy putting out fires in the **Urgent but Not Important** quadrant.

So how do you make time for the **Important but Not Urgent** stuff? Easy—you schedule it.

Get stuff done tip 4:
Create a schedule and stick to it

While researching his book 15 *Secrets Successful People Know About Time Management*, Kevin Kruse talked to hundreds of successful entrepreneurs and athletes about 'the secret of their success'. And what he kept on hearing was that if something was important to them, they scheduled time for it in their calendars.

Not *on* their to-do lists. *In* their calendars.

That's why I block out every morning in my week for writing and exercise. I used to wake up early in the morning, quickly check my email, and end up frittering away those precious hours responding to the 'urgencies' that landed in my inbox overnight. And when people got used to me responding to their 'urgencies' they'd send even more through during the night (rather than wait until the next day).

Lesson learned.

These days I don't answer any emails in the morning until I've done writing and exercise. And I try not to open my inbox at all on weekends because weekends are scheduled for family time, recharging and getting my house in order.

Remember how my morning routine gives me 45 minutes to have a shower, get dressed for the day and tidy the kitchen? What I'm doing is effectively scheduling a bit of whitespace into my day. Yes, I could 'quickly check my emails' or 'just put on a load of washing'. But doing so would introduce 'urgency' into my morning, and my goal of walking out the door feeling chilled would be torched.

So how do you create a schedule that lets you do these things?

Some people schedule their entire week: this block of time is for email, this day is product development day, this block is for phone calls, and so on.

My schedule is a little simpler: 4.30am-6.30am is for writing and exercise, 9.30am-2.30pm is for work. I have 2.30pm-4.30pm blocked out a few days a week for personal projects. And I've blocked out my daughter's sleep time of 1.30pm-4pm on weekends for me to either have a sleep as well or work on personal projects.

I also have certain times of each day blocked out as 'buffers'. This came in handy recently when I dropped my son to school and found out he had swimming lessons that day, but no swimming gear in his bag. I had time to make the 40-minute round trip home to grab his gear and deliver it to school and while I was irritated, it didn't detonate my whole day.

Get stuff done tip 5:
Set realistic deadlines

Another reason you might spend a lot of time in the **Urgent and Important** quadrant is that you're really bad at setting realistic deadlines. How do I know? Because that's exactly what I used to be like.

In the early years of my graphic design business I'd make the most ridiculous promises to clients. Every time they asked, "When can you have this done by?" my answer would be "Tomorrow". And because my point of differentiation was that I delivered on my promises, I basically spent every waking hour delivering on those promises.

Remember my moment of complete burnout that I talked about in the 'Passions' section? The reason I didn't have any time for my Passions is because I was too busy delivering on all the ridiculous promises I'd made.

Here's what you need to know about deadlines: People always want things done 'yesterday'. But they tend to adjust that expectation very quickly when they're forced to.

So force them to.

I won't lie—it will be hard at first. But the more you do it, the more you'll see how quickly people are willing to make that adjustment. And it will give you the confidence you need to be firmer and more realistic in the future.

Get stuff done tip 6:
Get off social media

I know—it's such an obvious thing. But something we all find ridiculously hard to do.

Earlier I mentioned Kevin Kruse, and how he talked to hundreds of successful entrepreneurs and athletes for his book *15 Secrets Successful People Know About Time Management*. He also spoke to more than 100 high-achieving students, and shared some of their time management secrets at the end of the book.

Pretty much every student mentioned social media, and shared tactics for managing the time they spent there. I was floored. But I shouldn't have been, because let's face it: It's what most adults do when they procrastinate these days.

Of course, we've always been able to find ways to avoid doing what we're supposed to be doing. Ten years ago we would have cleaned our houses or rearranged our desks. But while we could run out of things to clean, we'll never run out of things to look at on social media.

So how do you manage your social media time? Here's the method I use. If it works for you, great. If it doesn't, work out what does and implement it STAT!

I schedule time for social media—20 minutes in the morning and 20 minutes in the afternoon. Outside of those times I can only go on Facebook while I'm on my phone, which means I'm either killing time somewhere or lying on the couch chilling out. In other words, outside of the 40 minutes I've scheduled for it, I'm only on Facebook or Instagram when I'm not meant to be doing anything productive.

Get stuff done tip 7: Remove distractions

Phones ringing, emails pinging, message apps flashing— the potential for distraction these days is huge. We live in a society of instant gratification, and the need to be part of every conversation that involves us. So we set up notifications on our phones and computers to let us know about these conversations the moment they happen.

And we think we're really good at processing these distractions. The fact we didn't instantly reply to that Twitter mention makes us think we did a good job managing the distracting notification that just popped up on our phone. But we didn't, because having seen the notification we're now thinking about how to reply to it.

It's the same with email notifications quickly flashing up in the corner of the screen. We've seen who it's from, and maybe even the subject line. So even though we haven't opened the email to answer it, part of our brain is thinking about what we'll say when we do.

The easiest way to manage these distractions is to turn off notifications altogether. They don't just get in the way of work—they get in the way of life. If you've ever had coffee with a friend who loses track of the conversation whenever their phone starts flashing or buzzing, you'll know how sub-optimal those notifications are for proper human interaction.

So, I'll say it again: Turn. Them. Off.

You don't need to be notified the instant someone likes your latest photo on Instagram. You can find out how many people liked it when you log into Instagram.

Same with email. Stop the notification popping up in the corner of your screen. In fact, close email altogether while you're working on something important.

It's time to push back against our 'need it now' society. We've all been conditioned to expect an instant response to everything we do. Let's try to reverse that conditioning, and get back to doing what's actually important.

Get stuff done tip 8:
Stop multi-tasking

Ooh boy. If there's one thing us strivers pride ourselves on, it's our ability to multi-task.

But the fact is there's no such thing as multi-tasking. What we're actually doing is task switching: moving back and forth between tasks. And every time we move back and forth, we have to backtrack slightly to pick up from where we left off.

As John Naish points out in a piece for the Daily Mail:

> *"The human brain doesn't multi-task like an expert juggler; it switches frantically between tasks like a bad amateur plate-spinner."*[12]

An American study, reported in the *Journal of Experimental Psychology*, found that multi-tasking has a negative physical effect, prompting the release of stress hormones and adrenaline.

Multi-tasking can trigger a vicious cycle: We multi-task to get things done more quickly, but it ends up taking us longer. As a result, we start to feel stressed and harried, which compels us to multi-task even more.

Multi-tasking not only smashes our ability to be productive (reducing our productivity by 40%[13]), but also increases our cognitive load unnecessarily. We become tired more easily, and have less energy to get the tasks both done and done well.

The simple fact is that if we want to get tasks done quickly and efficiently, we need to stop splitting our brain and get back to single-tasking.

HOW MY LIFE GOT BETTER ONCE I GOT MORE PRODUCTIVE

I find there are few things more frustrating for me than getting to the end of a day where I have been busy, busy, busy, but feel like I've not achieved anything. And despite being a naturally productive person, this still happens to me a lot.

These days I know when I find myself in this hamster-on-a-wheel state, that the most important first step is to focus. Once I know exactly what it is I need to achieve in a given hour, day or week, then I can be more ruthless in shutting out distractions and staying on task.

I used the 'focus' tactic to write the first draft of this book. I then used it again to get through the editing phase which occurred while one of my kids was on school holidays. I've also used it to do mundane things like get my kitchen tidied in the evening so that when I finally sit down on the couch I can properly relax.

Most of all, however, Productivity makes my life better because it creates space in my life to just 'be'. That space fuels my creativity, makes me a better problem solver, increases my patience levels and in general, makes me a nicer person to be around. This isn't just good for me, but for everyone who comes in contact with me too.

MY CHALLENGE TO YOU

If there's one thing I want you to do, it's change your thinking on what the ultimate outcome of Productivity should be.

Most of us seek out Productivity as something that allows us to get more stuff done. I'd love you to instead choose to be productive in aid of creating more pockets of time in your day for meandering—the ability to move through your tasks in an unhurried fashion.

That distinction is crucial to the excellent life the Practical Perfection Framework is trying to achieve for you.

And now that we've covered the three key elements of the Practical Perfection Framework—Passions, Priorities and Productivity—it's time to talk about the one key element that binds them all together.

CONCLUSION

While I was writing this conclusion, Gretchen Rubin (author of *The Happiness Project*, *Happier at Home* and *Better Than Before*) shared one of her Secrets of Adulthood on Facebook.

"Accept yourself and expect more of yourself."

And it was so fitting because it neatly summed up an internal tension that strivers deal with every day.

We tend to be very good at *expecting more* of ourselves, but not so good at *accepting* ourselves. We hold ourselves to high standards (often without questioning whether they're reasonable), and then treat ourselves unkindly when we don't meet those standards.

This is what led me to where I found myself six years ago: stressed out, gripped by anxiety and depression, and wondering if it would be better for everyone if I wasn't in this world any more.

Clearly, life was far from perfect then.

These days, life still isn't perfect (because life isn't *meant* to be perfect). I still get stressed and anxious, I still fall into overwhelm and I still go through periods of time where I feel 'lost' and unproductive. The main difference between then and now, however, is I'm much better at being kind to myself when these things happen.

I'm much better at practising self-compassion.

WHAT IS SELF-COMPASSION?

Dr. Kristin Neff, considered the worldwide authority on this topic, says:

> *"... self-compassion means you are kind and understanding when confronted with personal failings ...*
>
> *You may try to change in ways that allow you to be more healthy and happy, but this is done because you care about yourself, not because you are worthless or unacceptable as you are. Perhaps most importantly, having compassion for yourself means that you honour and accept your humanness ... you will make mistakes, bump up against your limitations, fall short of your ideals. This is the human condition, a reality shared by all of us. The more you open your heart to this reality instead of constantly fighting against it, the more you will be able to feel compassion for yourself and all your fellow humans in the experience of life."*[14]

In short, self-compassion means offering the same kindness to ourselves that we extend to others. What's the number one thing that gets in the way of us being kind to ourselves? Our expectations of ourselves, and those high standards we're always striving for.

So how do we manage these expectations better? Well, we can start by better understanding how we, as individuals, respond to expectations.

Here's Gretchen Rubin again. While writing *Better Than Before* (her book about forming positive, lifelong habits), she identified Four Tendencies[15] in people when it came to expectations. (You can find out which one you are at *bit.ly/ HabitsQuiz*):

Upholder: describes those who respond readily to outer and inner expectations. (Outer expectations come from others (e.g. a deadline or a request from a partner), while inner expectations come from ourselves (e.g. a New Year's resolution or resolving to write a book in our free time).)

Questioner: describes those who question all expectations; they'll only meet an expectation (outer and inner) if they think it makes sense.

Rebels: resist all expectations, outer and inner alike.

Obligers: meet the expectations of others (outer), but struggle to meet expectations they impose on themselves (inner).

I'm an Upholder, and I suspect many of you are too even though Rubin says Upholders are rare.

Upholders are very self-motivated, and willingly rise to meet the expectations of both others and themselves.

Where we run into trouble is when we don't question the cost of rising to those expectations, or whether those expectations are reasonable.

If you're not an Upholder, and you're reading this book, then you're almost certainly an Obliger.

Where Obligers come unstuck is this: they get frustrated at never meeting the expectations they have of *themselves*, and irritated at how they always manage to meet the expectations of *others*. (Obligers are particularly prone to overwhelm.)

Meanwhile, if you're a Rebel or a Questioner, lucky you. You're far less likely to have heard the words "You're way too hard on yourself" and I'm amazed you're both reading this book, and have gotten all the way to the end!

I find Rubin's framework useful here because identifying which of the Four Tendencies applies to you makes you more aware of what drives your behaviour regarding expectations. As always, self-awareness is the crucial first step in making necessary changes in behaviour (the required change here being the need to show kindness to ourselves in the form of self-compassion).

Here's what strivers need to know about self-compassion:

- It doesn't mean we're lowering our standards.
- It doesn't mean we need to hold back from striving.

- It simply means we accept having finite resources (time, energy, support, patience) available to us at any given moment in time.

Self-compassion, to quote Theodore Roosevelt, gives strivers permission to:

"*Do what you can, with what you have, where you are.*"

HOW LIFE GOT BETTER WHEN I STARTED BEING KINDER TO MYSELF

Hmm. Where do I even start?!

Up until a few years ago my entire life was driven by the compulsive need to achieve. At school, in sport, as a friend, employee, business owner, boss, wife, mother; I had to be the very best I could be in every facet of my life. If I felt I wasn't meeting that standard, I got very down on myself.

Worse, even when I *was* achieving at the level I expected from myself, I never took the time to sit back and enjoy the 'glow' from those achievements. No, I was always thinking, 'Ok, box ticked. What's next?'.

It was exhausting. And very frustrating for the people who spent a lot of time with me.

Self-compassion only entered the frame when I went to therapy as part of my recovery from my breakdown.

Essentially, my therapist gave me the permission I seemed to need to be kinder to myself.

Since then, self-compassion has manifested in many different ways for me:

- I've gotten my head around the fact that I can't help every single person in the world and when I try to do that, my family suffer and I burnt out.

- I've gotten much better at saying 'no' to things that don't align with my stated core values because the alternative is constant overwhelm.

- I've learned to ask myself hard questions when I find myself in hamster-on-a-wheel mode. The answers to those questions usually tell me why I'm feeling a bit 'lost' in life.

Mostly, however, I've learned to cut myself slack when I fail to meet both the expectations of others, and those I have of myself.

Perhaps the best illustration of the above is this book. It's been in the works for three years and was originally slated to be published a year ago. For a variety of reasons, that just didn't happen but the main reason was, I couldn't get the bloody thing written! Instead of beating myself up for that however, I acknowledged the challenges that were getting in the way of me writing the book ... and gave myself permission to write it later.

And I'm glad I did. The book you are reading now is very different to the book that would have been written 18 months ago (in a good way). And I suspect the reason I am so proud of it is that it has come from a place of self-compassion.

SO WHERE TO FROM HERE?

I wanted this book to be a tool that helps striver types live the excellent life they desire. So it's probably worth quickly revisiting what strivers consider to be an excellent life.

It's one where:

- You can achieve the things you want to achieve without the constant stress and overwhelm that usually goes with being a person who sets high standards for themselves.

- You have time and space to be good to the people closest to you.

- You have time and space to be good to the world.

- You have time and space to be good to *yourself*.

I hope from this point on, whenever you feel a bit 'at sea' in life you can refer to the Practical Perfection Framework and clearly see what needs to change to bring you back to 'centre':

- Teetering on the edge of **burnout**? Now you know that ensuring there's something in your life that gets you out of bed with a spring in your step (**Passions**) might be just enough to pull you back from the edge.

- Feeling completely **overwhelmed** by everything life is throwing at you? You now know that bringing your **Priorities** into sharp focus will give you back that much-desired feeling of control.

- Finding yourself doing, doing, doing but never getting anywhere or achieving anything? You now know it's time to ensure you're not mistaking 'activity' for 'accomplishment', and that bringing greater **Productivity** to your life and actually finishing the things you start will be a truer measure of your 'accomplishment'.

But what if you're feeling more than one of these?

If that's the case, I suggest tackling them in the order they appear in this book: burnout first, then overwhelm, then 'hamster on a wheel'. (Whatever you do, don't try to take them all on at once. Trust me when I tell you it's futile.)

In the end though, the most necessary ingredient of an excellent life is the ability to be kind to ourselves and balance the expectations we have of ourselves with reality.

I hope this framework helps you practice better self-compassion, because that's what sets you up to be the person you most want to be: someone who can bring your best self to the world more often than not.

THE END

APPENDIX 1

I'm so grateful to Ellen Jackson from Potential Psychology who has gifted readers of this book the Values Exercise from her *Find Your Groove* Workbook.

Exercise: your values

On pages 117-119 you will find a list of words that describe commonly held values. Your task is to take a look through the list and circle those words that you feel apply best to you. Which words resonate with you? Which do you think are values that are important to you? Don't think too long or hard about it, just go ahead and pick a few.

When you're done, spend a few minutes thinking about how those values apply in your life. For example, a value of Family might influence the way you spend your weekends. Or a value of Economic Security might shape your decisions about work.

Make some notes about what the above tells you about your values:

_____

_____

_____

_____

APPENDIX 2

I am equally grateful to Lee Alexander from Brightside Coaching for allowing me to share the Core Values Exercise she uses in her program *The Flourish Project*®. I'll let Lee take it from here!

The benefits of understanding your core values

A key component in living a life that is truly yours is knowing your core values. Values are principles that you believe are important in the way you live your life. Values provide us with clear direction in our behaviour and decision making. Values-driven people find it much easier to prioritise their time and say yes to the things that fit, and no to those that don't.

When we are operating with no thought for our values we might feel empty, uneasy or anxious. It's good to listen to that unease and think about what value you might not be honouring to bring about that feeling.

So for example, if Environment is one of your core values and the organisation you work for actively damages the environment, you are going to be stressed and unsatisfied in your work.

Core Values Exercise

The following are some questions for you to work through. Take some time to do it, leave it and come back to it if you need to.

There is a list of values on pages 117-119. It is not an exhaustive list. You might have another word that is more suitable—please use whatever word you prefer.

Once you think you've settled on your core values it's a good idea to test them to see if they still feel right. They might take some trial and error or a particular experience to clarify them further.

Core Values Reflection Sheet

1. Think about three events/ successes/ accomplishments that you are most proud of in your life.

_____

_____

_____

2. What values are you demonstrating by highlighting these events?

_____

_____

_____

3. Think about difficult times in your life. What values were being trodden on?

_____

_____

_____

4. Think about times in your life when you felt satisfied and fulfilled and most "you". What values were being honoured?

_____

_____

_____

5. Now I want you to form a short list of 8-10 values. You can use the list on pages 117-119, go off the top of your head or use Google.

Values shortlist

1. _____

2. _____

3. _____

4. _____

5. _____

6. _____

7. _____

8. _____

9. _____

10. _____

6. Now I want you to narrow it down to 5 Core Values.

1. _____

2. _____

3. _____

4. _____

5. _____

7. Now put your values in order, with the value you hold most dear to you as number one.

1. _____

2. _____

3. _____

4. _____

5. _____

VALUES LIST

Acceptance	Diversity
Accomplishment	Economic security
Achievement	Education
Acquisition	Effectiveness
Adventure	Elegance
Alignment	Emotional wellbeing
Altruism	Empathy
Amusement	Encouragement
Attractiveness	Energy
Authenticity	Enlightenment
Awareness	Entertainment
Beauty	Environment
Being	Equality
Calm	Ethics/Ethical
Charity	Excellence
Community	Experience
Compassion	Experiment
Connection	Expertise
Consciousness	Exquisiteness
Consideration	Fairness
Constancy	Faith
Contentment	Fame
Contribution	Family
Cooperation	Feeling good
Courage	Fitness
Creativity	Freedom
Danger	Friendship
Daring	Fun
Dependability	Generosity
Dignity	Grace

VALUES LIST CONTINUED

Gratitude
Happiness
Harmony
Health
Honesty
Honour
Hope
Humility
Imagination
Improvement
Independence
Influence
Inner peace
Innovation
Inspiration
Integrity
Intelligence
Inventiveness
Joy
Justice
Kindness
Knowledge
Laughter
Leadership
Learning
Love
Loyalty
Magnificence
Mastery

Merriment
Nobility
Nurturance
Observation
Order
Organisation
Originality
Peace
Peacefulness
Perception
Personal Development
Play
Pleasure
Positive attitude
Power
Preparation
Presence
Proficiency
Provider
Quest
Radiance
Recognition
Relatedness
Relationships
Relaxation
Reliability
Religious/
Religion
Resourcefulness

VALUES LIST CONTINUED

Respect
Responsibility
Responsiveness
Risk
Safety
Schooling
Self-awareness
Self-worth
Sensations
Sensuality
Serenity
Service
Simplicity
Spirituality
Stability
Stimulation

Strength
Success
Superiority
Support
Teaching
Touch
Tranquility
Trust
Truth
Understanding
Victory
Vision
Wealth
Wisdom
Zeal
Zest

REFERENCES

1, 2. Timothy A Pychyl Ph.D., April 30 2008, **What Flavor of Perfectionist Are You? It Matters!**, *Psychology Today*, psychologytoday.com/blog/dont-delay/200804/what-flavor-perfectionist-are-you-it-matters.

3. William MacAskill, December 2015, **The Many, Many Problems With "Follow Your Passion"**, *99u.com*, 99u.com/articles/51623/the-many-many-problems-with-follow-your-passion.

4. Joshua Fields Millburn and Cal Newport, **'Follow your passion' is crappy advice**, *theminimalists.com*, theminimalists.com/cal/.

5. Mark Manson, October 22 2015, **Screw finding your passion**, *markmanson.net*, markmanson.net/passion.

6. © Elizabeth Gilbert, September 22 2015, *Big Magic*, Bloomsbury Publishing Plc.

7. Oliver Emberton, **How to find your passion**, *oliveremberton.com*, oliveremberton.com/2014/how-to-find-your-passion.

8. David Brooks, 12 April 2015, **The Moral Bucket List**, *The New York Times*, nytimes.com/2015/04/12/opinion/sunday/david-brooks-the-moral-bucket-list.html

9. Wikipedia, **Fear of missing out**, *Wikipedia*, en.wikipedia.org/wiki/Fear_of_missing_out

10. Author Unknown, **Why think about values?**, *Brunel University, West London Website*, brunel.ac.uk/pcc/secure/Destinations/units/unit-v006.shtml

11. Nicole Avery, *Planning With Kids*, planningwithkids.com

12, 13. John Naish, August 11 2009, **Is multi-tasking bad for your brain? Experts reveal the hidden perils of juggling too many jobs**, *The Daily Mail Australia*, dailymail.co.uk/health/article-1205669/Is-multi-tasking-bad-brain-Experts-reveal-hidden-perils-juggling-jobs.html

14. Kristin Neff, April 2011, *Self-Compassion. The proven power of being kind to yourself*, William Morrow

15. Gretchen Rubin, January 14 2015, **Ta-Da! The launch of my quiz on the Four Tendencies. Learn about yourself!**, *gretchenrubin.com*, gretchenrubin.com/happiness_project/2015/01/ta-da-the-launch-of-my-quiz-on-the-four-tendencies-learn-about-yourself

ACKNOWLEDGEMENTS

To Bernadette Jiwa—for the amazing book title, sorting my brain out and pointing out what should have been obvious (but the obvious seldom is, right?!). Anyone whose life is impacted positively by this book owes you a debt of gratitude.

To Gabbi Armstrong—for working through three different book titles, seven different outlines and the need to talk me off the ledge a good few times. This book wouldn't have gotten over the line if not for your friendship, support, structural advice and much-valued second pair of eyes.

To Bill Harper, my editor—it is always such a relief to place a manuscript in your hands and know it's going to come back 100 times better.

To Kym Campradt, never are your eagle-eyed proofreading skills more needed than when I can't help but keep editing right to the death. Which is what I did!

To Ellen Jackson and Lee Alexander, thank you so much for allowing me to share your 'value-finder' exercises in the appendices of this book.

To the advance readers who provided incredible and valuable feedback: Anthony Exeter, Bernadette Jiwa, Theresa Andrews, Meryl Johnston, David Tiong, Michelle

Elizondo, Linda Manson and Jane Newman. Thank you for making this book better.

To Emma Isaacs, William MacAskill, Cal Newport, Mark Manson, Oliver Emberton, Kirsten Neff and Gretchen Rubin—thank you for letting me share your thoughts and words. Thank you also to Bloomsbury Publishing for permission to publish the short extract from Elizabeth Gilbert's *Big Magic*.

To all my A *Life Less Frantic*® blog readers and Facebook followers—this book is the six years of writing I've done for you, distilled into 120 pages! Thank you for always being frank about what resonates with you (and what does not). This book has been shaped by you guys more than anyone else.

To Jaden and Mia—the love I have for you scares me senseless. And provides incredible drive to do my bit to make the world a better place.

And finally, to Ant—it's not easy being married to someone who likes to live in their head. Thank you for patiently coaxing me out into the real world each day.

THANK YOU

As a fellow reader with limited time on my hands, I know what it's like to commit to a book, long or short. If you've got this far, I'm honoured and appreciative that you've gifted your time to me. I hope you enjoyed *Practical Perfection*.

If it sparked something for you, please drop me an email at kelly@kellyexeter.com.au, I love to hear which bits resonate with each individual as it seems to be different for everyone.

And if you'd like to stay in touch, I'd love that too! You can:

Get weekly tips for living A Life Less Frantic®
at kellyexeter.com.au

Say hi on Facebook (facebook.com/kellyexeter),
on Twitter (@kellyexeter),
or Instagram (@kellyexeter.
(I love seeing beautiful flat lays of book
on Insta #justsaying.)

Thank you again!
Kelly x

37742065R00075

Made in the USA
Middletown, DE
01 March 2019